EDGE
BOOKS

✦ INTO THE GREAT OUTDOORS ✦

BOWHUNTING
For Kids

BY MELANIE A. HOWARD

Consultant:
John Schlieman
Certified Bowhunting Instructor, State of North Dakota
Life Member, North Dakota Bowhunters Association

CAPSTONE PRESS
a capstone imprint

Edge Books are published by Capstone Press,
1710 Roe Crest Drive, North Mankato, Minnesota 56003.
www.capstonepub.com

Library of Congress Cataloging-in-Publication Data
Howard, Melanie A.
Bowhunting for kids / by Melanie A. Howard.
p. cm. – (Edge books: into the great outdoors)
Includes bibliographical references and index.
ISBN 978-1-4296-8424-8 (library binding)
ISBN 978-1-4296-9265-6 (paperback)
ISBN 978-1-62065-223-7 (ebook pdf)
1. Bowhunting–Juvenile literature. I. Title.
SK36.H69 2013
799.2'15–dc23   2012006893

Editorial Credits
Brenda Haugen, editor; Ted Williams, designer; Marcie Spence,
    media researcher; Sarah Schuette, photo stylist; Marcy Morin,
    scheduler; Laura Manthe, production specialist

Photo Credits
Alamy: parm, 21; Capstone Studio: Karon Dubke, 1, 3, 7, 9 (background),
10-11, 16, 18, 22, 24, 26, 27; Corbis: Bettmann, 9 (inset); iStockphoto:
Mur-Al, cover; Shutterstock: Al Parker Photography, 4-5, dcwcreations,
15, Laborant, design element, Marcel Jancovic, 14, Sergey Kamshylin, 13,
Wesley Aston, 29

Printed in the United States of America in Stevens Point, Wisconsin.
032012   006678WZF12

TABLE OF CONTENTS

It's your third day out from camp. You picked up the trail of a black bear halfway through day one. Yesterday you found a bunch of raspberry bushes where the black bear has been returning to eat. Now it is time to sit and wait.

Every time you hear a rustle in the brush, your hand tenses around your bow. To your disappointment, it always turns out to be a chipmunk, squirrel, or bird. As the light begins to fade, a rabbit hops past. You wonder if you'll ever see the bear.

Then, as though by magic, the bear appears. You hold your breath, trying not to make a sound. If the bear hears you, it will spook and run. It will even run away if it smells you. But you're prepared. You make little noise as you draw your bow. You're focused on making the perfect shot.

Your bow is aimed at the bear's chest. You take a deep breath, relax, and release the string. The string twangs. The arrow strikes. With a startled snort, the bear runs off. The arrow is stuck deep in its side.

You wait an hour and then begin to track the bear. A blood trail leads you to the body lying near the raspberries. The bear is already dead, a reward for all of your practice with your bow and arrow. You will not need to use the shotgun you brought along. Your bow shot was clean and true. This bear will make an excellent trophy.

FACT
Bowhunters must get close to the animals they plan to hunt. A bow and arrow's range is only about 45 yards (41 meters).

Weapon of Choice

Hunters have been using the bow and arrow for thousands of years. Guns were not used for hunting until the 1500s. Today bowhunting is a sport enjoyed by nearly 3 million Americans.

Why bowhunting? Many hunters say they switched from rifle hunting to bowhunting for the added challenge. Some people like the connection to traditional hunting. Others say they enjoy spending more time in nature in order to take game. Many bowhunters point out all these reasons and more.

A VARIETY OF TARGETS

Animals that are commonly bowhunted:

- deer
- bears
- turkeys
- moose
- sheep
- wild hogs

FACT
For thousands of years, American Indians used bows and arrows to hunt buffalo and other animals.

CHAPTER 2

BOWS AND OTHER GEAR

Hunting with a bow and arrow is a challenge. Bowhunters work to improve their **archery** skills all year long. It takes strength to **draw** a bow. It takes even more strength to hold a drawn bow steady. There can be more than 80 pounds (36 kilograms) of force pulling against your muscles, depending on the bow.

Choosing a bow that works for you is the most important decision you will make in bowhunting. And there are many bows from which to choose.

TAKING AIM

When first learning archery, you need to know which eye is your aiming eye. To do this, make a triangle with your pointer fingers and thumbs. Hold the triangle out in front of you, and stare at an object a distance away. Slowly bring the triangle back toward your face, keeping your eyes on the distant object. The triangle should come to rest over your aiming eye.

archery—the sport of shooting at targets with a bow and arrow

draw—to pull back

Longbows

Until the 1930s, hunters and archers used only longbows for their sports. A traditional longbow is made of one piece of wood and is very tall. The English longbow is the average height of a man. Of all bows used today, the longbow requires the most strength to draw.

Longbows need a lot of care. They must be stored unstrung. They should be stored at a constant temperature to protect the bow.

Recurve Bows

The recurve bow has a long history. It was used for fighting on horseback thousands of years ago. But its history in modern hunting is much shorter. Around 1930 the recurve joined the longbow on the hunting scene.

A recurve is smaller than a longbow. The recurve gets its name from its ends, which curve out when the bow is drawn. Early recurves were made of animal **sinew**, animal horns, and wood or bamboo.

sinew—a strong piece of body tissue that connects muscle to bone

The modern recurve is made of wood, plastic, and fiberglass. Fiberglass is a strong, lightweight material made from thin threads of glass. Unlike a longbow, a recurve is not affected much by temperature and humidity. A recurve also can shoot farther and more accurately than a longbow, and it takes less effort to use.

recurve bow

compound bow

Compound Bows

A compound bow is the easiest bow to use. It was first used in the 1960s. Today more than 90 percent of bowhunters use compound bows. Because it uses a system of wheels and cables, a compound bow takes less strength to hold in the drawn position than other bow types. It is more accurate and powerful than longbows and recurves.

Crossbows

Some hunters use crossbows. But crossbow hunting often has different rules than other types of bowhunting. In some states, using crossbows is illegal. In many other states, crossbows can be used only by hunters who are disabled. A crossbow's bowstring is drawn back by a special device and locked into position. Shooting a crossbow is much like shooting a gun. That is why it's often illegal to use a crossbow to bowhunt.

crossbow

Gear and Gadgets

Bowhunting keeps getting more popular. As a result, there is more equipment available to help with your hunting trek. Gloves, finger tabs, and release aids are standard equipment for most bowhunters. Gloves and finger tabs protect your fingers from the bowstring. A release aid protects your fingers too, but it also helps you make a steady, more accurate shot. An arm guard is needed too. It protects your arm from the bowstring.

FACT
A powerful bow will make noise when the string is released. This sound could scare game away. A string silencer is a good gadget to have to keep your bow silent.

Most bowhunters use a sight, a device that helps them aim better at their prey. Sights come with pins or crosshairs. Most bowhunters use a fixed-pin sight because pins can be added and removed as needed. Many hunters combine their mounted sight with a peep sight. A peep sight forces you to keep your head in one place, which makes your shot more accurate. Bowhunters also use **arrow rests** to aid their shooting accuracy.

Bowhunters use many of the same gadgets rifle hunters use. A range finder allows a hunter to determine the distance between his or her position and the prey. This is really important in archery, because the arrow drops dramatically in flight. Knowing the distance helps a hunter make sure that an arrow is aimed correctly and will not end in a miss or a bad hit. You can even buy special unscented wash and body soap. They help keep game from picking up a hunter's scent.

arrow rest—a device that helps hold an arrow in place when shooting a bow

CHAPTER 3

STANDS, STALKING, AND STILL HUNTING

Once you have all your equipment, it's time to decide what method of hunting works best for you. This is often a question of where and what you are hunting. But personal preference also comes into play. Often methods are combined during the hunt.

Stands and Blinds

A stand is elevated, usually in a tree. A blind is on the ground. Other than that, the idea is the same. A hunter waits behind a blind or in the stand for the game to come by. The hunter uses the **camouflage** of the blind and the elevated position of the stand to stay hidden from game.

These are very popular hunting methods, but they're not as simple as they sound. A good hunter needs to be aware of wind direction. If the wind starts blowing toward your prey, the animal could pick up your scent and be scared away. Hunters often have more than one stand set up so that if the wind changes direction, they can move downwind.

camouflage—coloring or covering that makes animals, people, and objects look like their surroundings

Still Hunting, Stalking, and Glassing

Still hunting, stalking, and glassing are done on the ground and involve movement. Still hunting is a way of moving through the hunting area very slowly with many pauses. You are trying your best not to make any noise. Because of the many pauses and slow pace, it could take an hour to cover 100 yards (91 m). Still hunting usually works best in forests or places with dense cover.

The stalking method is used in more open country. You can see the prey. The prey can also spot you. The idea of stalking is to slowly approach the prey until you get close enough to shoot it. As with still hunting, you use what cover there is and stay downwind. You try not to alert the animal to your movements.

Glassing is hunting using a scope or binoculars. You use the gadgets to spot the prey from a distance. Then you stalk it.

BOWFISHING

Many bowhunters also enjoy bowfishing. Much of the equipment for bowhunting is the same for bowfishing. You still need a bow and an arrow. You also need a reel mounted on your bow. The line in the reel attaches to the arrow.

A bowfisher must account for refraction, or the way light bends when it hits water. The fish isn't where it looks like it is from above the water's surface. You may need to fire 6 inches (15 centimeters) below where it looks like the fish is to strike it. Then reel it in!

Calling and Baiting

Calling and baiting are usually done to draw game to a certain place while a hunter waits in a stand or behind a blind. A call is a recording or other device that mimics a sound that will draw game to your position. There are four kinds of game calls: a distress call, a position call, an aggression call, and a mating call. Each one mimics a different kind of sound. If you want to use a call, check your state laws first. Some states only allow calls blown with a person's mouth.

Baiting can be as easy as putting out a salt lick. Some hunters spread corn around an area or dump it in a pile. The animal comes to the food, offering the hunter a clean shot. But check your state laws before baiting. Quite often it is illegal to bait for animals. Plus, many hunters do not consider baiting to be **sporting**.

sporting—in line with the ideas or rules chosen as the fair way to perform a sport

Safety and **conservation** are important topics for hunters. The idea of fair game and sportsmanlike behavior run deep in the hunting world. It is important to know the rules of your state and to follow them.

Safe Hunting

Most states require hunters to wear blaze orange during firearm hunting season. But many states do not require bowhunters to wear blaze orange during archery or bowhunting season. This is because bowhunters must be closer to their targets to shoot them. Bowhunters do not often accidentally shoot people. But accidents do happen. Many people argue for and against wearing blaze orange. Statistics show that it does save lives. Either way, always be sure of what you are shooting at before releasing an arrow.

When shooting, be very sure that your lane is clear of people. Never shoot in the direction of a person, no matter how sure you are that you won't hit them.

conservation—the protection of animals and plants, as well as the wise use of what we get from nature

Bows are not considered as dangerous as firearms. But you should still be sure to use them safely. Make sure your arrows are stored safely in the **quiver**. If one pokes out, it could hurt you or someone else.

quiver—a container for arrows

quiver

mosquito hat

If you have a longbow or other bow that you store unstrung, be very careful when stringing it. It could spring up and injure you. You should also always make sure your bow is in good condition and your string is not frayed. You could get a nasty welt when a frayed string snaps. It is also a good idea to wear the proper protective gear, such as gloves and an arm guard, when shooting.

Wilderness safety is also a concern. A first-aid kit is a must for any hunting trip. A survival kit is also a good idea. Good footwear, mosquito protection, sunscreen, the proper clothing for the weather, and water are also needed.

Rules for a Reason

Hunters are limited on the number of animals they can shoot in a season. Why are there so many limits when it comes to hunting? Without limits, there is a danger of hunting animals until there aren't any more left.

The Department of Natural Resources sets the hunting seasons in each state based on the animal population. The goal is always to have a healthy population.

Hunters who break the rules usually face fines and lose their hunting licenses for periods of time. They are also frowned upon by other hunters who follow the rules. Most hunters are very passionate about conservation. They want game to be plentiful for a long time to come. With healthy animal populations, hunters can continue enjoying their sport.

FACT
The passenger pigeon was hunted to extinction in the late 1800s and early 1900s. It has since become a symbol for conservation.

GLOSSARY

archery (AR-chuh-ree)—the sport of shooting at targets with a bow and arrow

arrow rest (AYR-oh REST)—a device that helps hold an arrow in place when shooting a bow

camouflage (KA-muh-flahzh)—coloring or covering that makes animals, people, and objects look like their surroundings

conservation (kahn-sur-VAY-shun)—the protection of animals and plants, as well as the wise use of what we get from nature

draw (DRAH)—to pull back

quiver (KWIV-ur)—a container for arrows

sinew (SIN-yoo)—a strong piece of body tissue that connects muscle to bone

sporting (SPOHR-ting)—in line with the ideas or rules chosen as the fair way to perform a sport

READ MORE

Gross, W.H. "Chip." *Young Beginner's Guide to Shooting and Archery: Tips for Gun and Bow.* The Complete Hunter. Minneapolis: Creative Publishing International, 2009.

Gunderson, Jessica. *Bowhunting for Fun!* For Fun. Minneapolis: Compass Point Books, 2009.

Peterson, Judy Monroe. *Big Game Hunting.* Hunting: Pursuing Wild Game! New York: Rosen Central, 2011.

INTERNET SITES

FactHound offers a safe, fun way to find Internet sites related to this book. All of the sites on FactHound have been researched by our staff.

Here's all you do:

Visit *www.facthound.com*

Type in this code: 9781429684248

Check out projects, games and lots more at
www.capstonekids.com

INDEX